Zoo Vet Alphabet

The Animal Adventures of Dr. Scott Amsel

Sheri Amsel

Published by
Exploring Nature Educational Resource
PO Box 84, Elizabethtown, NY 12932
www.exploringnature.org

Acknowledgments

We'd like to thank Dr. Peregrine Wolff, friend and colleague, for taking many of the amazing photos used in this book, the Los Angeles *Zoo for permission to use the "lizard-gizard-wizard", Ruth LaBarge for letting us photograph Betty and Alleyoop at her bear preserve, Curt LoGiudice for the opportunity to photograph his many beautiful and happy "cats" at the Catty Shack Ranch Wildlife Sanctuary and Hayden Rosenaur for letting us photograph his African elephants at Serengeti Ranch. We also appreciate the many volunteers who took shots at just the right moments to make this book possible.*

ISBN 978-1523826926

There is a vet named Scott Amsel,
who works to make all creatures well.
So turn the pages and you'll see,
his patients lined up A to Z.

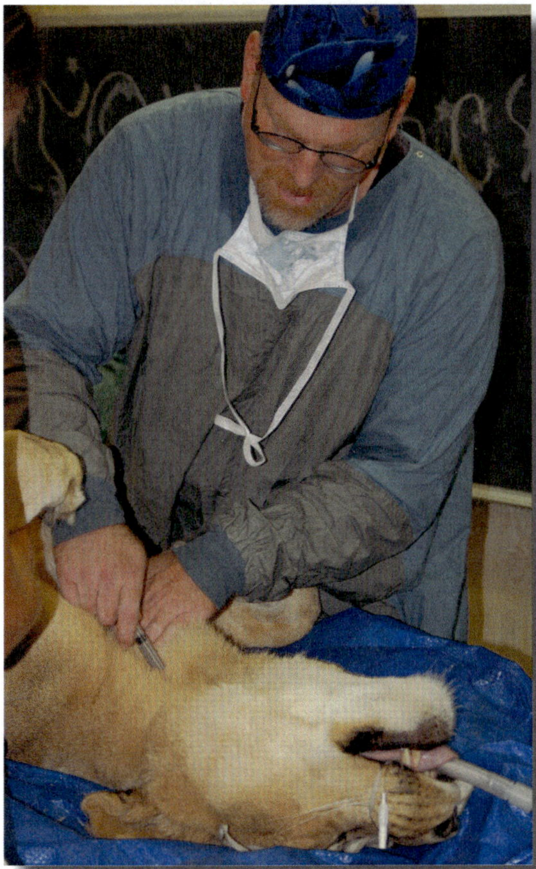

A baby **A**pe, not at his best,
is resting on the doctor's chest.
When he grows up, he'll someday be,
a strong and handsome chimpanzee.

A

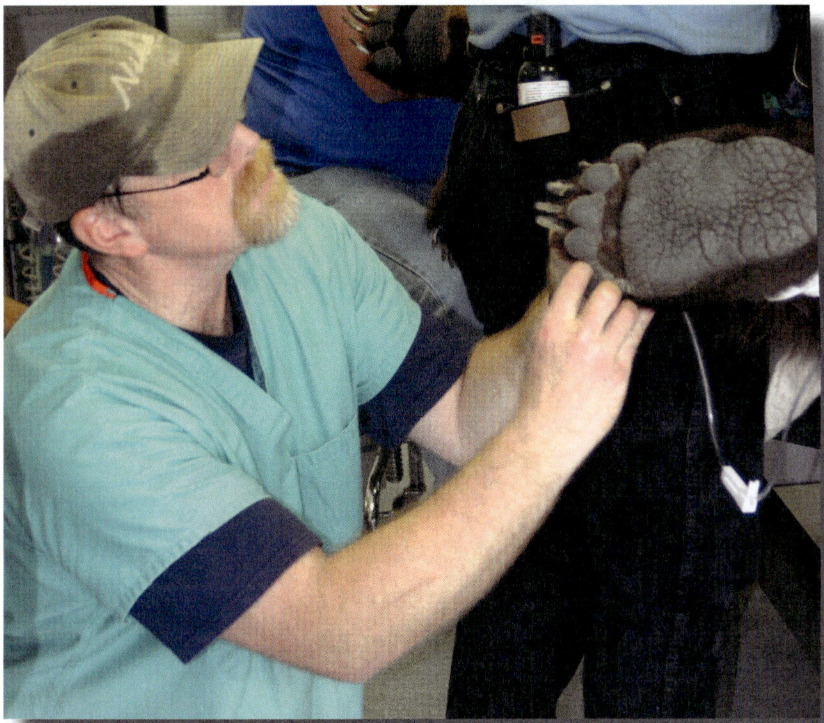

B

A **B**lack **B**ear's paw gets checked above.

A **B**aby **B**ear gets doctor's love.

The **C**oatimundi
left her pen
and would not
get back in again.

They Chased her – she was really fast,
and caught her with a net at last.

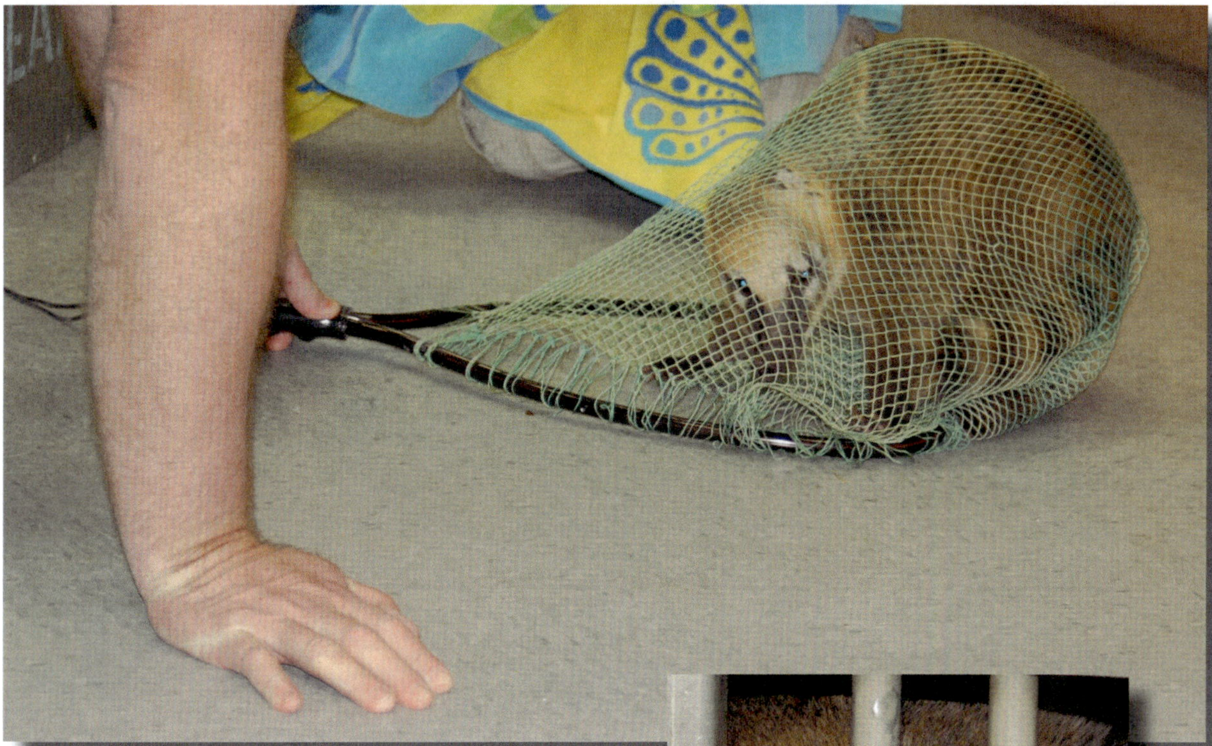

After treatment she went home,
where she could run around and roam.

D

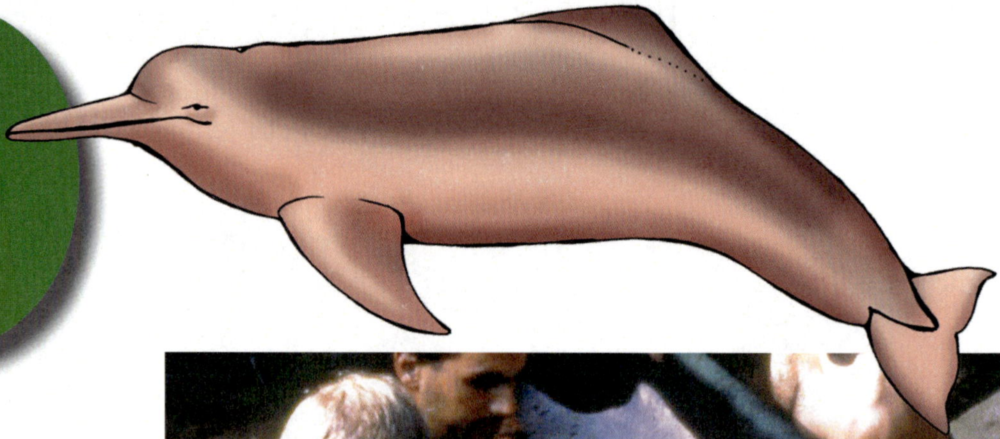

A river **D**olphin
colored pink,
is not as
strange as you
might think.

While Scott
was working in
Brazil,
he cared for
one that was
quite ill.

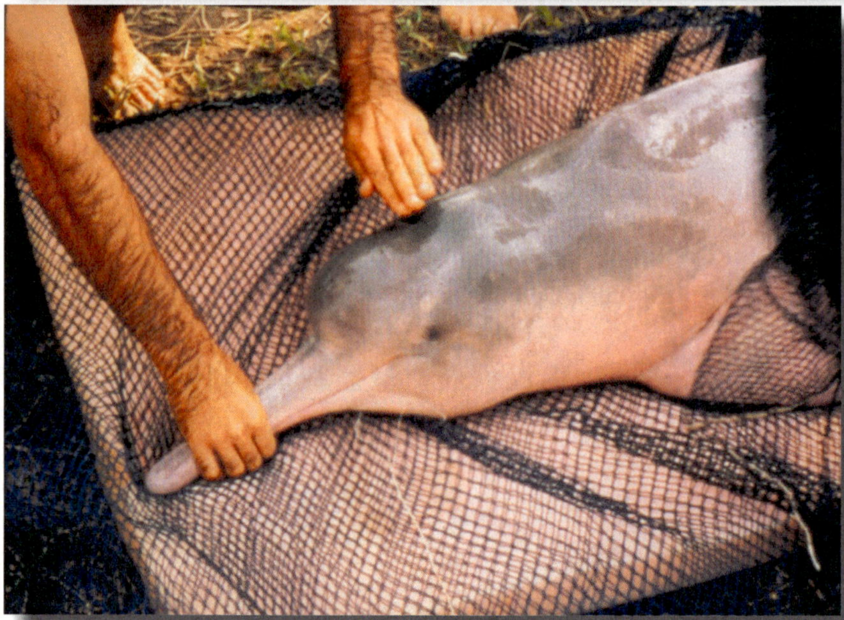

D

Though **D**ogs are not found at the zoo,
they can be lifelong friends to you.
Wherever Scott has made his home,
he's always brought his **d**ogs along.

Elephants at a petting zoo,
can a have a real effect on you.
This little pachyderm he met,
would make Scott want to be a vet.

E

F

A **F**erret who was losing hair,
recovers with some food and care.

G

A **G**ecko with a bellyache,
is very ill, his life's at stake.
The surgery that saved the lizard,
made Scott a lizard-gizzard-wizard.

H

Hippos are a danger zone.
Back away. Leave them alone.

Scott treats an **I**guana with a smile,
and looks inside the small reptile.

J

This **J**aguar has a toe infection.
It will need a close inspection.

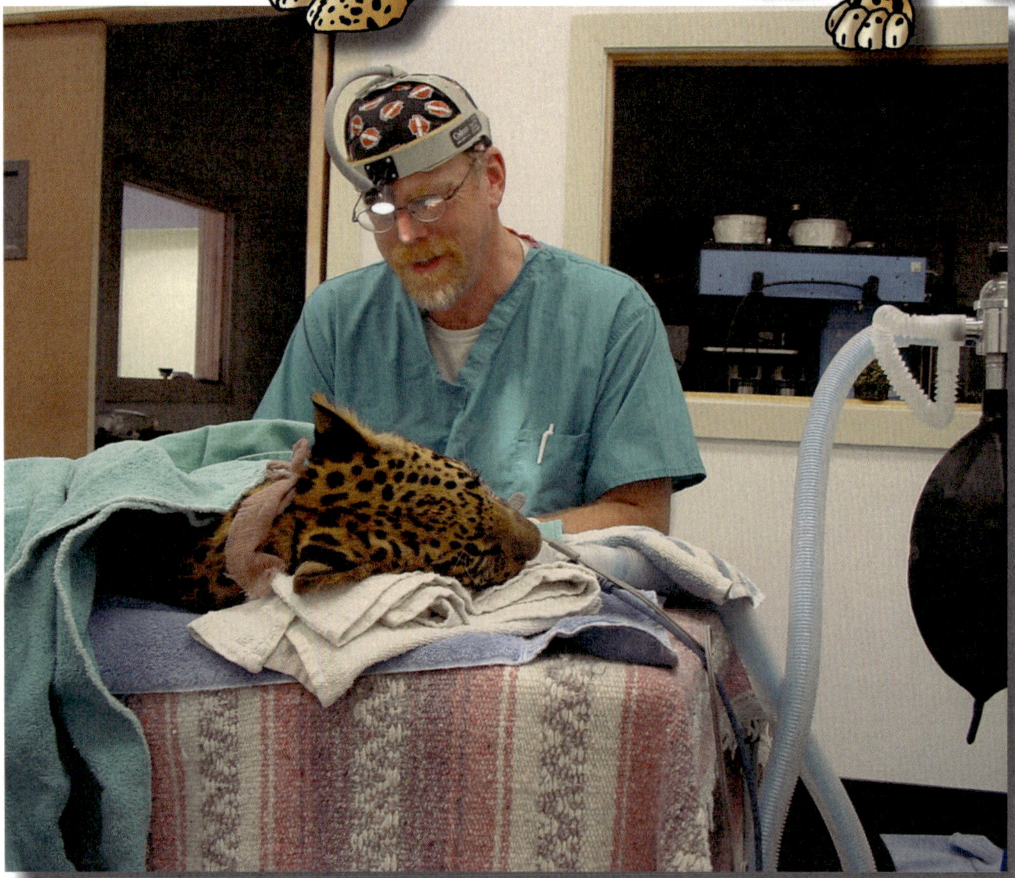

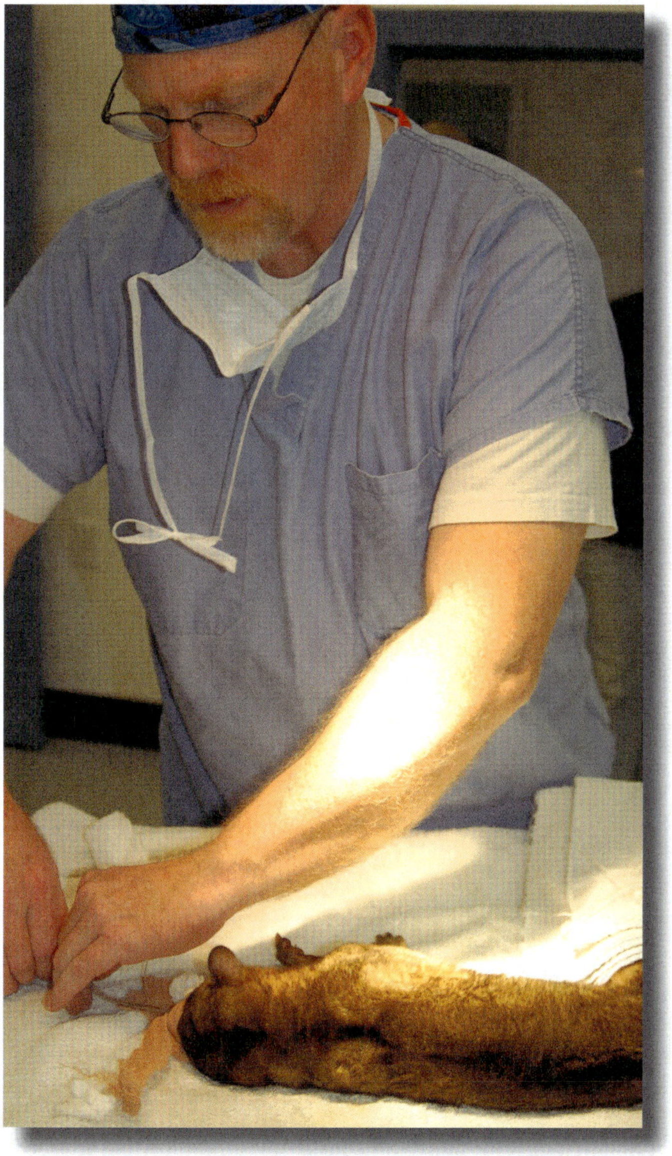

The **K**inkajou is
off his feet.
They monitor his
strong heartbeat.

K

Baby Tapirs look quite weird,
But like to **K**iss the
doctor's beard.

L

The sleeping Lion opens wide,
and shows her canine teeth inside.

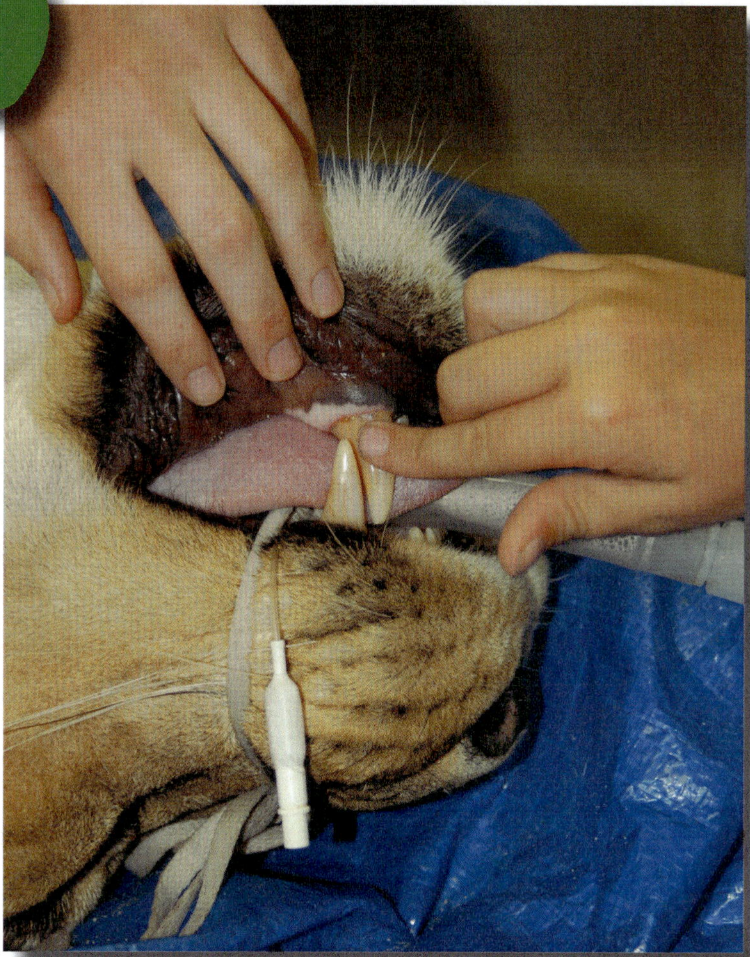

The **L**ynx is having breathing tests.
He'll feel better once he rests.

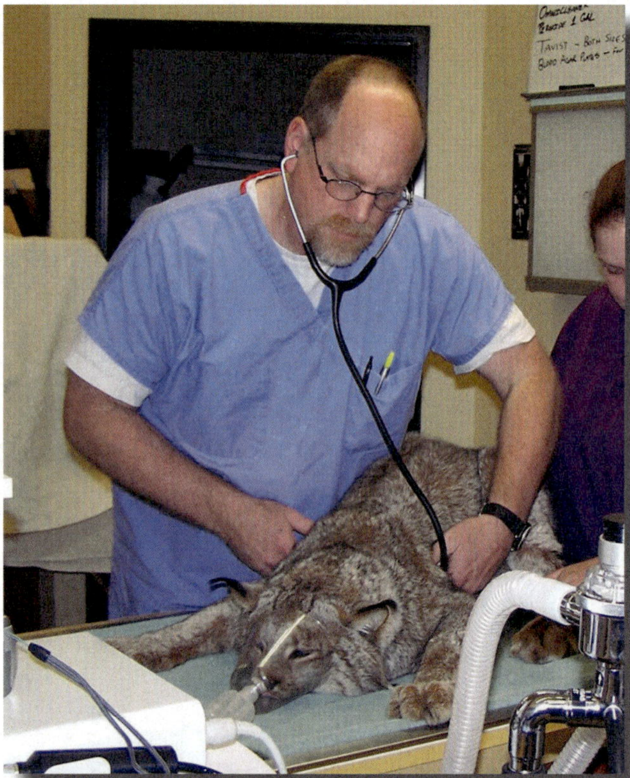

M

A **M**onkey and a gibbon play,
Which helps these primates
learn each day.

In the **N**ursery
come and see,
a baby sloth that
clings to me.

O

Orangutans with
bright red hair,
are rescued and
need loving care.

P

A **P**uma lying in
a heap,
will get a check
up while asleep.

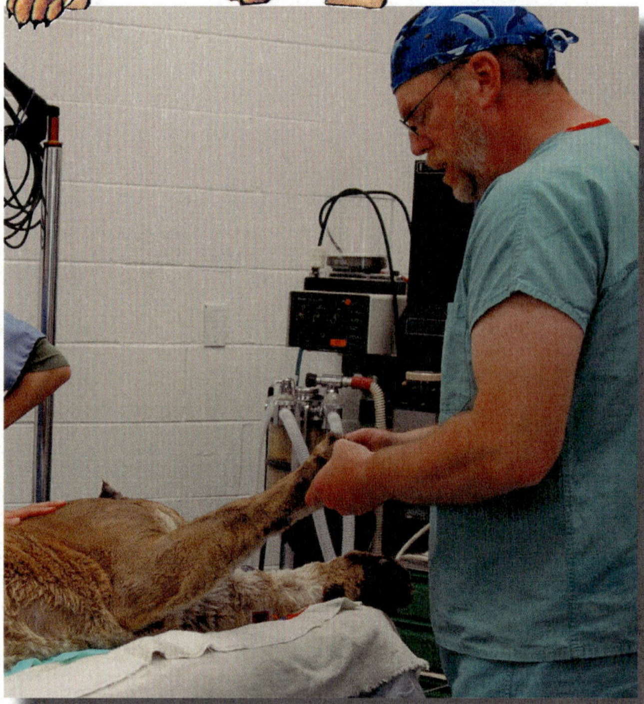

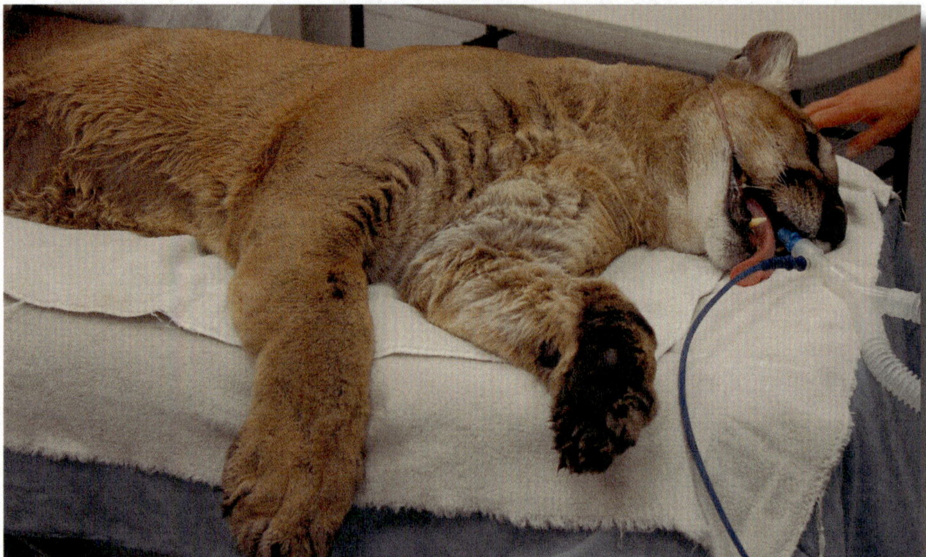

A coat of **Q**uills,
will work just fine,
as armor for a
porcupine.

But it's a risk when
one gets sick,
to check its health
without a nick.

R

A giant **R**hino loves to eat,
So Dr. Scott gives him a treat.

Though **S**kunks may have a stinky spray,
it will not keep the vet away.

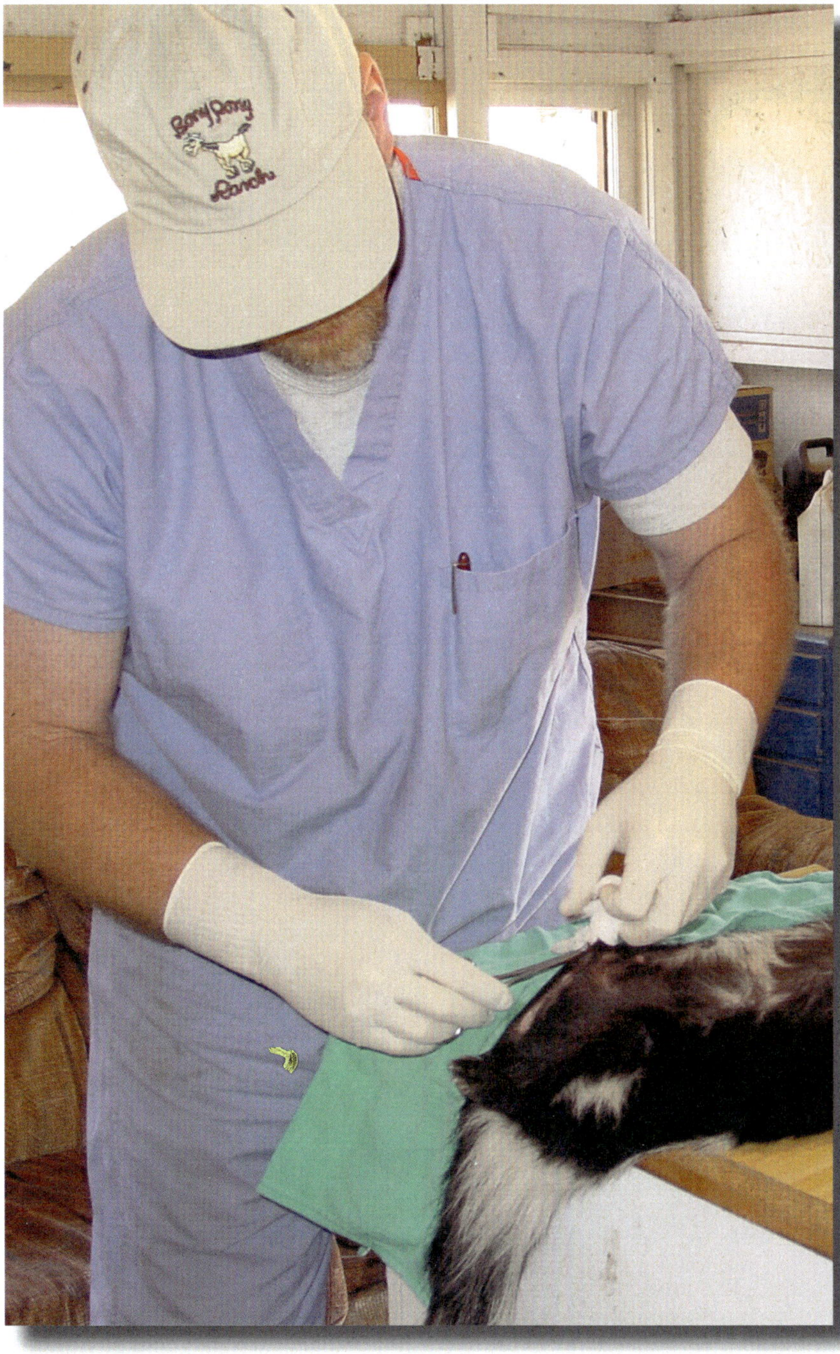

S

Snow Leopards are a cat so rare,
that treating them demands great care.

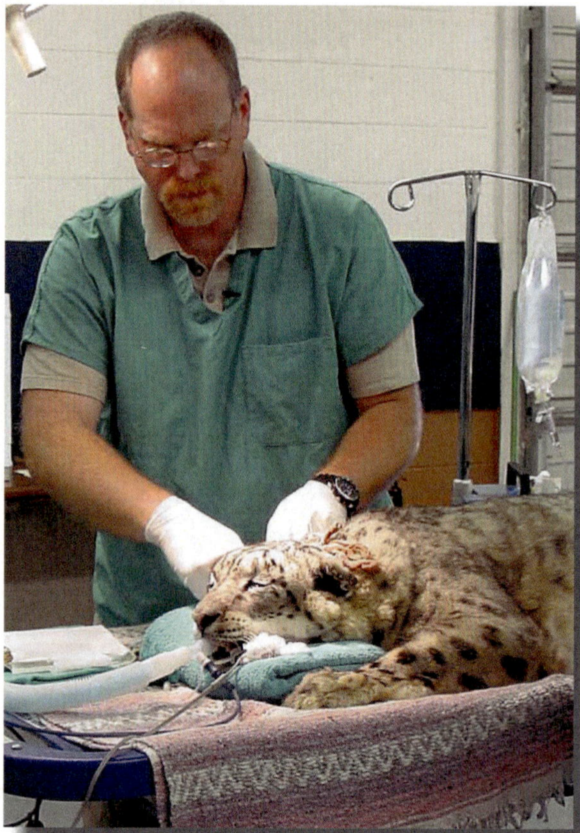

To cure a day that's gone a muddle,

Try a baby Tiger cuddle.

T

T

The playful Tiger had a sore,
that Dr. Scott could not ignore.
He cleaned it up and then he dressed it,
hoping she would try to rest it.

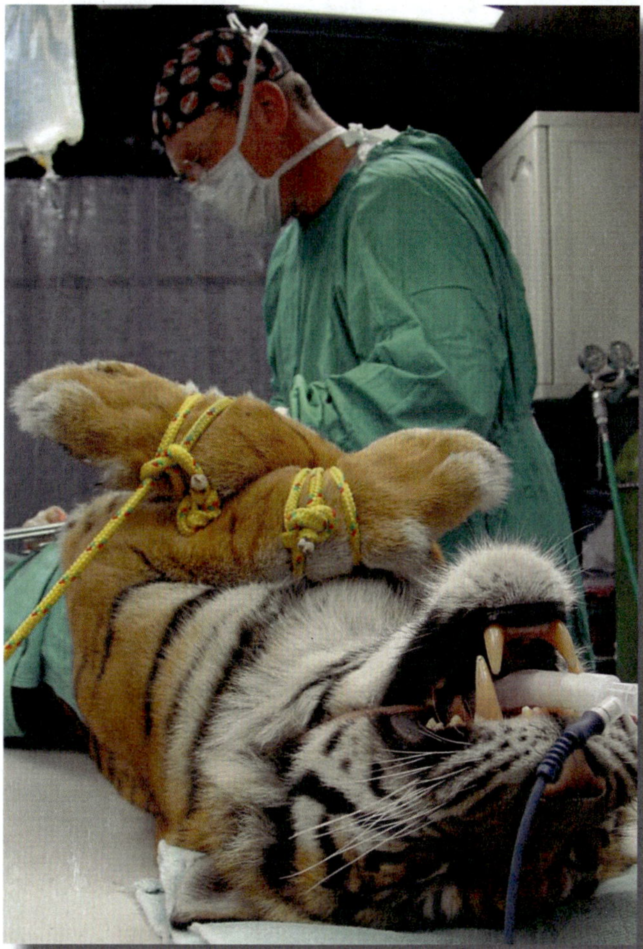

Underwater, Scott took meals,
to sting rays, turtles, fish and eels.

U

V

Because a Zoo **V**et can get hurt,
when treating tigers, STAY ALERT!
Injecting big cats, show no fear,
and always shoot them in the rear.

W

A broken foot –
one out of four.
This **W**olf will be a little sore.

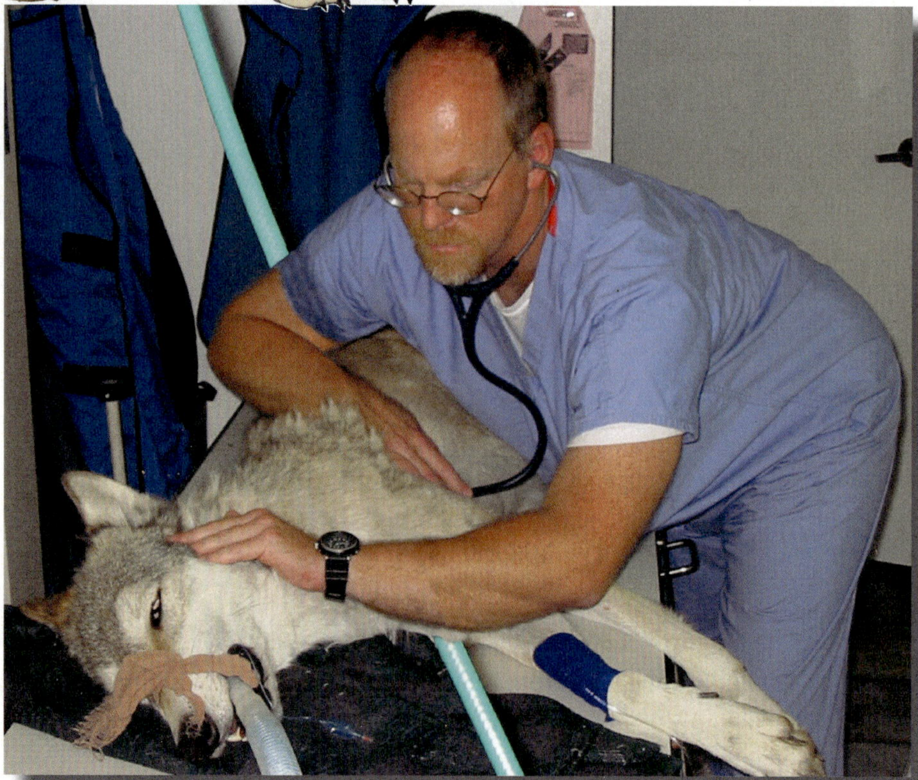

X

The X-ray on the viewing screen,
reveals a break that's
small and clean.

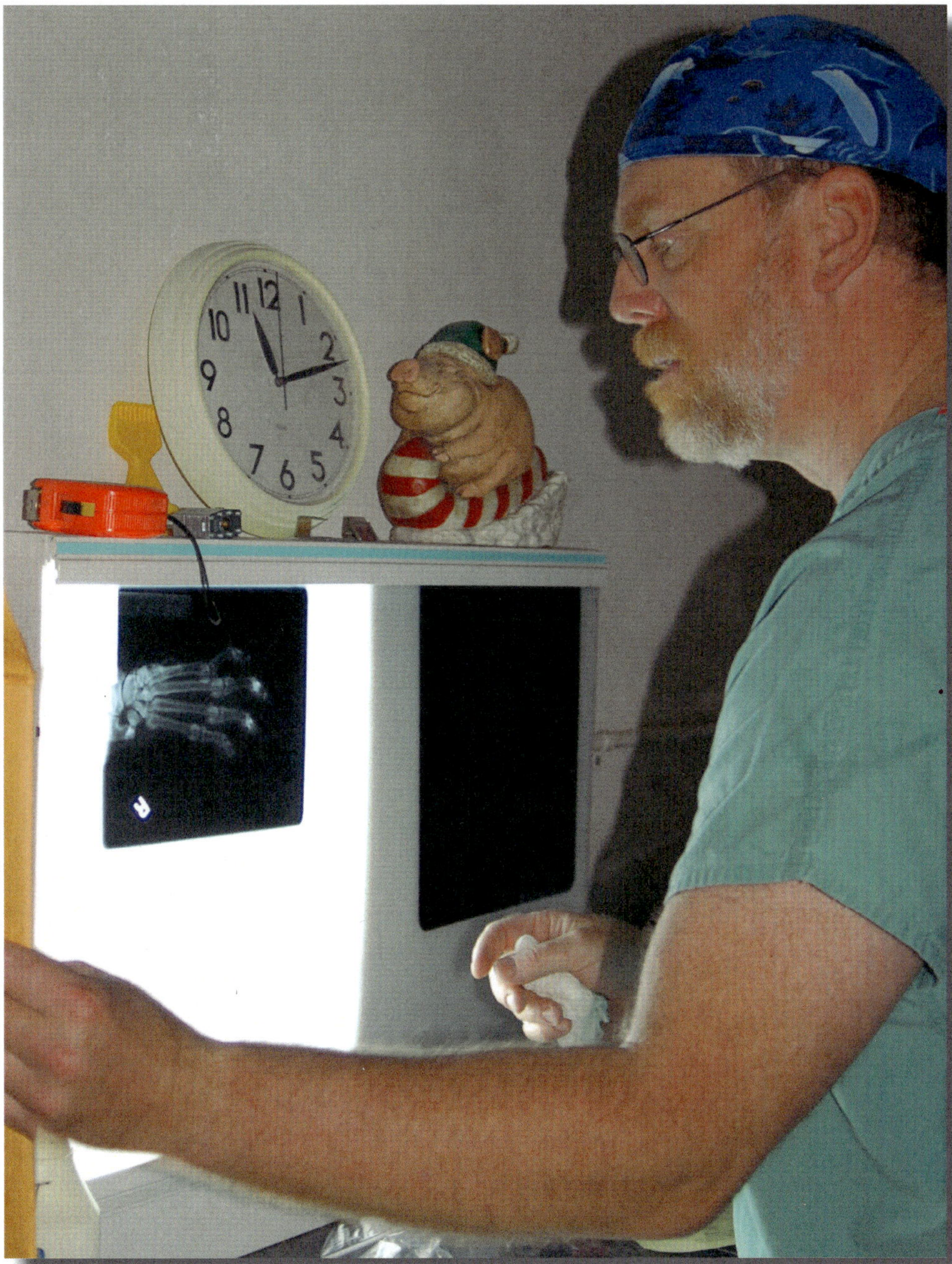

Y

A Yowling leopard
makes a face....

Z

The **Z**oo's a wild
and noisy place.

A B C D E F G

APE

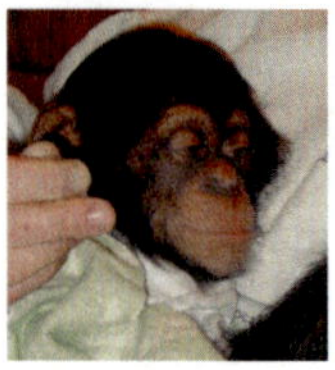

BEAR

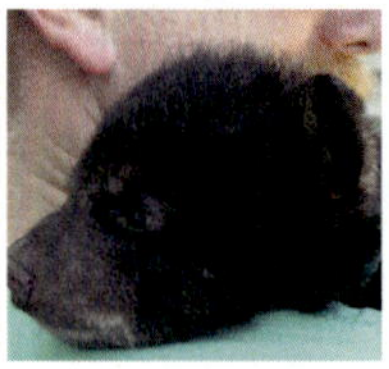

COATIMUNDI

DOLPHIN

ELEPHANT

FERRET

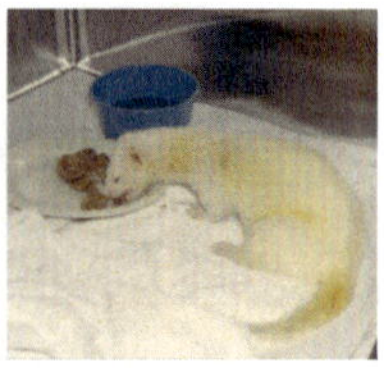

GECKO

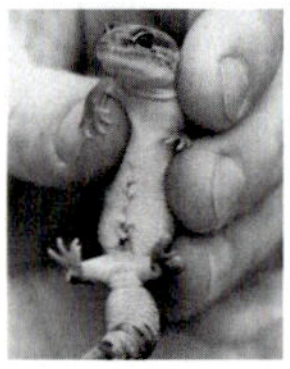

H I J K L M N

HIPPO

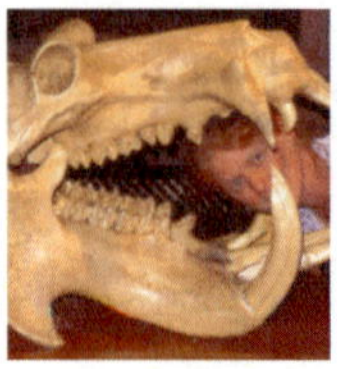

IGUANA

JAGUAR

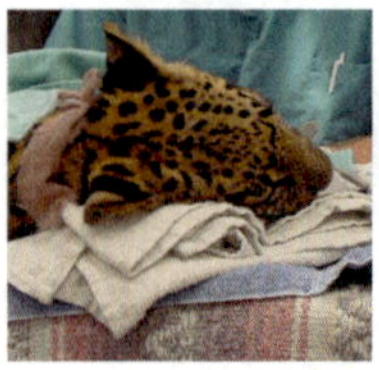

KINKAJOU

LION

MONKEY

NURSERY

O P Q R S T

ORANGUTAN

PUMA

QUILLS

RHINO

SKUNK

TIGER

U V W X Y Z

UNDERWATER

VET

WOLF

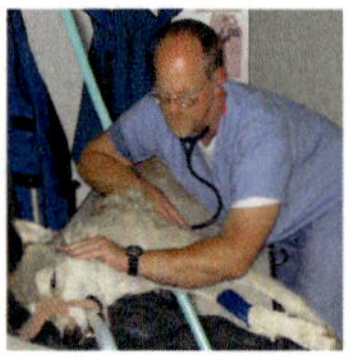

X-RAY

YOWL

ZOO

Photo Credits

Page 1 - Scott drawing blood from lion at Catty Shack, Jacksonville, FL. Photo by Sheri Amsel.
Page 2 - Scott and baby chimpanzee. Photos by Dr. Peregrine Wolff.
Page 3 - Scott and black bear and Scott and black bear cub. Photos by volunteer.
Page 4-5 - Scott and Coatimundi. Photos by Sheri Amsel.
Page 6 - Amazon River dolphin Dolphin. Photo by a volunteer.
Page 7 - Scott and dogs. Photo by a friend.
Page 8 - Amsel family at petting zoo in 1960. African elephant photo by Dr. Scott Amsel taken at Serengeti Ranch.
Page 9 - Ferret photo by Sheri Amsel.
Page 10 - Gecko photo from the Los Angeles Zoo. Photo by staff photographer.
Page 11 - Hippo Skull photo by Laurel Amsel.
Page 12 - "Jaguar" Photo by Dr. Peregrine Wolff.
Page 13 - Kinkajou and Scott. Photo by a volunteer.
Page 14- Tapir and Scott. Photos by Sheri Amsel.
Page 15 - Lion canines at Catty Shack, Jacksonville, FL. Photo by Sheri Amsel.
Page 16 - Lynx and Scott and Lynx sleeping. Photo by Dr. Scott Amsel and volunteer.
Page 17 - Baby apes photos by Dr. Scott Amsel.
Page 18 - Baby Sloth photo by Dr. Scott Amsel.
Page 19 - Orangutan photos by Dr. Scott Amsel and a volunteer.
Page 20 - Mountain Lion and Scott. Photos by volunteer and Dr. Amsel.
Page 21 - Porcupine photo by Sheri Amsel.
Page 22 - Scott with rhinoceros. Photo by Sheri Amsel.
Page 23 - Scott and skunk. Photo by a volunteer. Sheri with skunk. Photo by Dr. Amsel.
Page 24 - Snow Leopard and Scott. Photo by Dr. Peregrine Wolff.
Page 25 - Scott with tiger cub. Photo by Dr. Peregrine Wolff.
Page 26- 27 - Tiger Photos by Dr. Scott Amsel, a volunteer, and Sheri Amsel (respectively).
Page 28 - Scott diving. Photo by a friend.
Page 29 - Scott giving tiger injection. Photo by a volunteer.
Page 30 - Scott with wolf. Photo by a volunteer.
Page 31 - Scott looking at x-ray. Photo by a volunteer.
Page 32 - Yowling leopard at Catty Shack, Jacksonville, FL. Photo by Sheri Amsel.
Page 33 - Standing grizzly - Photo by Dr. Scott Amsel.
All illustrations by Sheri Amsel.

About the Veterinarian

Dr. Scott Amsel received his veterinary degree in 1984, while specializing in the study of zoo and wildlife medicine at the University of California Davis. Scott's career has taken him on many animal adventures around the world from working in the Amazon with wild river dolphins to caring for rescued and rehabilitated orangutans in Indonesia. Scott was staff veterinarian at the LA Zoo and Disney's Animal Kingdom in Orlando, Florida.

His ongoing exotic animal work includes caring for grizzlies, elephants and tigers for a series of wildlife facilities and acting as "vet on the set" for television programming. Scott regularly helps to dart feral dogs for rescue and placement in loving homes. He lives in Northern California with his beloved canine family.

About the Author

Sheri Amsel has written and illustrated more than 25 books for children. Sheri received a master's degree in anatomy and biomedical illustration from Colorado State University, where she worked with the veterinary school on an illustrated guide to llama anatomy.

Sheri's work includes writing and illustrating children's books and field guides, school and library programs, outdoor education, and the development of illustrated science resources online. She has accompanied Dr. Amsel (her brother) on many excursions to animal facilities to document his work. This book is the result of those adventures. Sheri lives in upstate New York with her husband and big, brown dog. You can see her work on **Exploringnature.org** and **Coloringnature.org**.

31995162R00024

Made in the USA
San Bernardino, CA
25 March 2016